The Shape of Water

Swimming Poems

by Andy Skitt

Copyright © Andy Skitt 2021

For Julia and the Flamingos

The Shape of Water

– A swimming pool love story in 4 poems

The shape of water

He turns
   pushes from the side
      and glides before
         the surface breaks a fluid-locked silence

      She relishes the anonymity
     of the high gallery
      each Tuesday and Friday lunchtime
    as she watches

    counting off his strokes and lengths
    measuring the twist of shoulders
    waiting for him to pull himself
     up onto the tiles and search for a towel

     There is embrace in her landfooted status
      a non-swimmer squirming to follow in his wake
     get to where he's been before the space fills
   and becomes water again

At half past one
  she drifts towards Tesco
    to get oven chips
     for her torpid supper

   and as he slouches
    back to an idling laptop
  she follows for a while

occasionally close enough to rest her foot

on his shadow

The Reshaping of Water

He is mid forearm in Marigolds
   not listening to Radio 4
      not wishing for a dishwasher

This is wallowing sink-time
  first rinse
    set the piles left
  then the glasses
    bowls above plates
    cutlery soaks in a saucepan
as he runs the hot
  squirts Fairy Lemon
    and begins the wash

The mandate of actions
  allows thoughts to trickle
    into spume-filled dreams
  as idle minutes
    sluice through suds
  and onto the drainer
before he finishes
  with a swill of the bowl
    and wipes down worktops
  Intermittently
he speculates
  whether the woman
    sitting in the mezzanine seats
    during his lunchtime swims

   has noticed him

      crawling the liquid lanes

      or hauling out

   into dryness

   His relaxed reflection

      in the oven door

      causes him

        to hold a breath

   tilt back shoulders

      and pull in stomach

     before

      reaching

   for the tea towel

The unshaping of water

He tucks the yellow t-shirt
   a little tighter
      enhancing the precision
   of repped biceps
   and a worked-on torso

Some swimmers
sneak a look at him
   faux slouched
      on the raised chair
  above the deep-end
as he twitches pecs
   and dreams
      of a life
  as bare-chested lifeguard
on a Cornish summer beach

   He knows the habits
  of these bathers
names them for their days and times
   colour of cap and suit
   or preference of stroke

   He surmises about absentees
   the unexpected meetings
minor illnesses
and two-week jaunts
   by a hotel pool

So speculation is piqued when

    40-lunchtime-lengths

    Man

is not in the water today

    but is in the gallery

  laughing at something

    Hiding-behind-a-magazine

    Woman

  has said

    as their hands engage

Water finds its own shape

She slides back the shower screen
    steps in as his eyes close
        against the shampoo sting

Arms wrap around him
   wetly whispering
that he is getting more cuddly

    Although he laughs
he thinks of the swimmer's body
she fell in love with

    The steaming cataract
  rinses his thoughts into her
    and she enfolds him

      says   yes
        it was his selkie sleekness
      along the pool lane

      but also
    how he joked with the chatting
    tandemswim ladies

    waited
      as the amateur triathletes
      tumble turned

    how he signalled

    to the posturing lifeguards

       as he dripped to the changing room

      how he looked at her watching him

      and smiled when she first

       caught his eye

He kisses her beaded forehead

  asking

     if he can wash her hair

Sirenstrokes – 14 Wild Swimming Poems

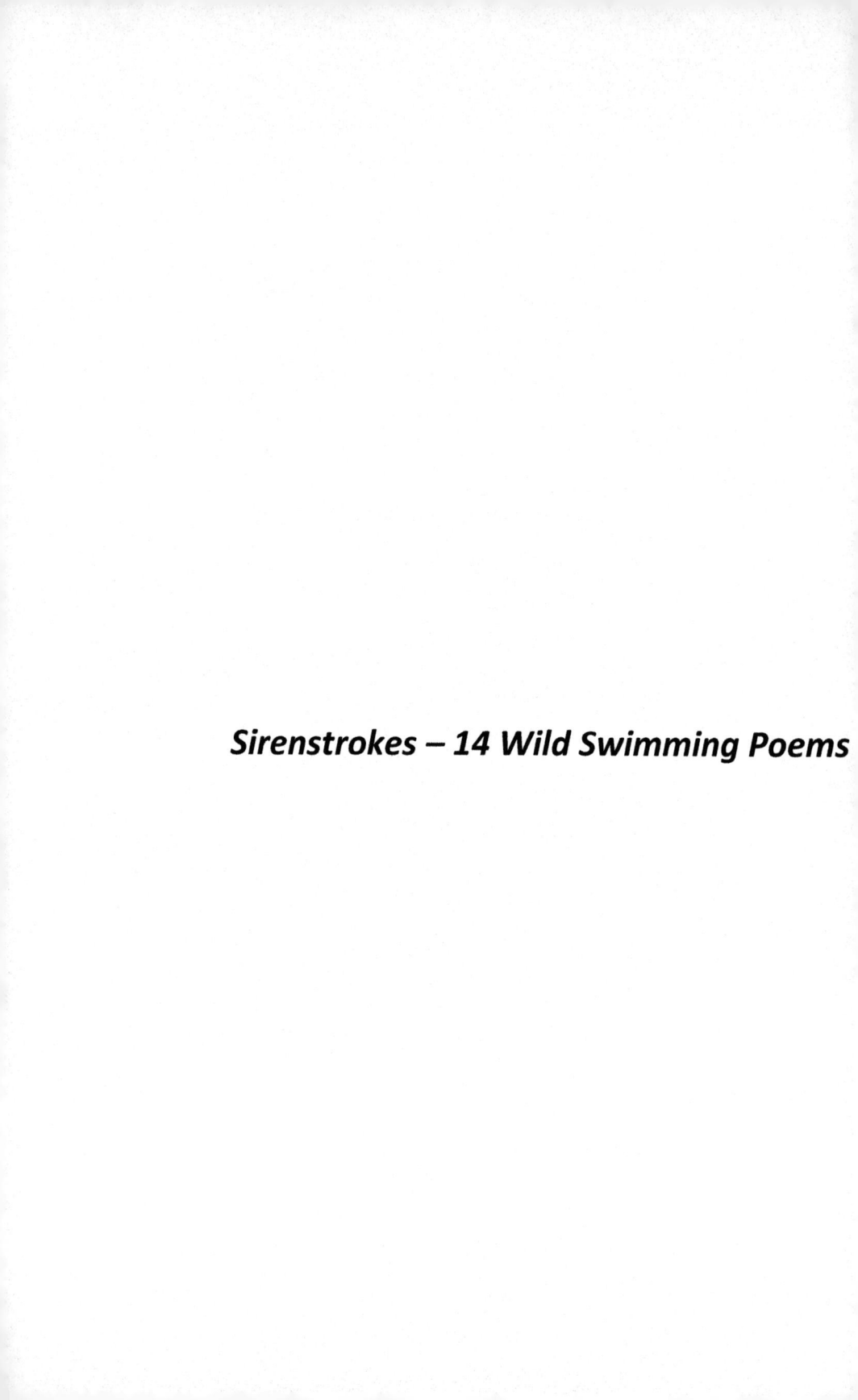

Llyn Eiddew-bach

There is the walk
    up deepening furrows
    of farm track

There is the mud
    re-ignited in its wetness
    by a week of rain

There are the clouds
    glowering
    like a schoolyard bully

There is the wind
    more needling
    the higher they climb

There is the fact
    that this tarn promises
    to be over the next ridge

    and then isn't

    But at last
there is rawloveliness
of water and slate crag

    There is a stripping away
of protecting layers
    a tentative tilt of bare foot on rock

    And there is the cold
oh
the cold

    the breath squeezing
skin ripening
cold

Bala

Early mizzle
has mustered

breaks the
unexcited

tension of
lake surface

    Stretch arms
      pull back

    and stroke
    from shore

First
swim

after winters
coldwater pause

means resisting
siren call

of dayglo
mooring buoys

   keeping depth
     measuring breath

and waiting
for reason

to flex
back in

Ardnave Point

    Naked on white sand

  Before me
the darkening definitions
 of Mull
      Jura
          Colonsay
cradle the tail
 of the North Atlantic Drift

This water
      now lapping my ankles
  tells ocean-stories

  and as I step deeper
my body feels
for the residual warmth
    of equatorial seas

 but finds instead
    the restoration
   of a skin-prickling
  Hebridean reality

Llanbedrog

        Dead jellyfish almost sway us
but the sea is calm and empathetic

  In the settling of evening
     only dog-walkers
       distract themselves on the sand

So we swim
    gasping
     prattling
      and wary

Endorphins kick in
I snicker
     at the mountains
     the oystercatchers
     the statue of the iron man
         profiled high on the headland

Laughter stops
as something translucent
     floats past my elbow

    I splash it away
as some nebulous sea-lore
    whispers
     about creatures that sting
        even in death

Bruichladdich

Sea-pink headland
sun kicks away from tacky clouds
   a beach looking semi-tropical

      The water
         teasingly
      feels more arctic

Wading out sees us more
   overlooked than we assumed
      when we decided to skinny-dip

A minibus on the road
      pauses
two smartphones point my way

I dither
   between brazen and coy
then wave before dunking

hoping they are not
   now taking a vote
      about whether to join us

Llyn Hafod-y-lly

Trees surround the water
       when we are in
             leaf-rotted lakebed
       spongily retreats under feet

Ramblers
   twitchers
     and steam train buffs
watch with amused
but indulgent disbelief
     as they huddle deeper
     into scarves
and fur trimmed collars

We scull and float
   hear a semibreve toot
     the force of steam
     leaving brass and copper
and through the trees
   see plumes
     white against the tipping
     of autumn

I scent
   condensing heat
     swirl my hands
     swim a few strokes
under the canopy
of stripling silver birch
     and imagine the
   triune state
of completing ice
with a succeeding season

Loch Gearach

She floats in a scintillation of nothingness
    loch water is peaty
        velvety
            the colour of a smoky dram
  and buoys her
     unwearying body

The sun casts off
from the harbour of morning clouds
    and she sculls
       slowly rotating
           lining up her toes
       with surrounding hills

    giggling
at how the sky
and water have become one

leaving her to hover
   like a hen harrier in
      an offshore breeze

ThomaSON Foss

                                            He is taller than me now
takes the lead as the path dissolves
so we slither towards the reverberation
of falling water

                  Ignoring the rope swing
we crab over submerged rocks
until they disappear
into the coldblack plunge pool

The head emptying sound
triggers primal terrors
we swim nearer
forcing through the needling screen

breathing
but not breathing

gasping
at voluntary waterboarding
as we pull onto the narrowrock ledge

He yells
BRAINFREEZE
and I acknowledge the sensation
before we erupt through the icy curtain
startling the dipper on the rock
just below our folded clothes

As I try to climb out
my knee groans and locks
and he offers a hand

I catch a glimpse of him
        four years old
lifted over the shushing waves
on an evening beach

Llyn Gwynant

The weather
        and gravity
defeat us

Waterfalls
on the Watkins Path
do not look
as idyllic
as promised

and to bathe
in the plunge pools
would need recklessness
        ropes
        harness
        and helmet
none of which we possess

So the wide lake
        shallow where we pick our way in
                the mountain
        reaching up on the far shore
is where we skinny dip

Entering one by one
        white backsides
                barely hidden
                from passing traffic
        wobble then tense
        before disappearing
        into freshly tumbled water

Port Charlotte

He swims to the
mooring buoy
   flouting the elastic security
     of sand
        tethered toes

Below him
the depthdarkening
      swirls
   with imagined dangers
and the illogical fears

    that without warning
       he will develop
     an anvil buoyancy

    and the prospect
       in this taciturn sea loch
   there lurks something
     that may
   want to eat him

Kings Cross Pond Club (2016)

        Breath leaves
    and enters
at the same time
        heart rate spikes
      skin contracts and pinks

Within a few strokes
the tenderness of water
     warms   like an Emperor's
  new dressing-gown
and you become a pallid seal
       twisting
     floating
   gawping
at the October sky
   framed by high rise flats
and construction cranes
    the colour of flamingos

Within the stretching breadth
you hear   shouts   sirens
 a city growing and shifting

      Closer in
splashed conversations
between swimmers
    comparing
coldwater places
 where they have
   tipped back their heads
   and sculled away
from the comfort
    of humanity

Porth Dinllaen

They dip next to the lifeboat station
        the sea   shallow and soundless

Across the bay
he can make out the cottage
where he holidayed
for most of his teenage summers

      The path to the beach
        winding a hairpin way
      down the cliffs

        Solitary
         pre-breakfast walks
      picking shells and stones
           a beauty lost
            in dry pockets

He floats
      pondering
         advice to be shouted
         across water and time

  The cars to avoid
  The jobs to stick at
  The realities of love

  That the seas won't forever
    be calm
     and a lifeboat
  is always the last resort

Hay-on-Wye

The proprietor of the Poetry Bookshop
looks sceptical
when I say I'll swim in the river
then return later   to browse and buy

I follow a narrow path
  onto the high riverside
below me
   the drift is wide and slow
    a fleet of hired canoes
   zigzag a disorderly
      tilting voyage
        from drop-off to pick-up

At a shingled meander
   aware that I am being watched
   by temporary inhabitants
   of the holiday let
   on the far bank
I forge in

I swim against the tender flow
   then turn and glide
  past rucksack
 clothes
and shoes
  before I put down my feet
   push back upstream
     and do it again   and again
    until the chill slinks deeper

'There is a collection
  about wild swimming'
    he says when I return
'but I don't have it in stock'
 I'm washed by
   disappointment and relief
     but see that he is
    unconvinced
    when I tell him
   the water was lovely

Traeth Penllech

Death took me by the hand today
        showed me
        how easy it was
        to hurtle into a blue embrace

Death plunged me out of my depth today
goaded the undertow
        to drag me
beyond the hint of feet on life

Death filled my throat with brine today
        crashed me with brimstone
          bile and the reflux
        taste of hell

Death was half-hearted today
        trusted autumn winds and dark tides
not reckoning
   on the other decrees

Death was brutish today
battered my skull with noise
        then shruggingly accepted
            that within an hour

            I would be dry and silent
                pen in one hand
                glass of rippling
                single malt in the other

Printed in Great Britain
by Amazon